Famous

"A *tour de force*...these poems are crafted
in order to reward us with new senses of
perspective—as only exceptional poetry can do."

Dick Allen
Poet Laureate, State of Connecticut
2010 Harriss Poetry Prize Judge

Famous

Bruce Sager

Winner of the Harriss Poetry Prize
Michael Salcman, Prize Series Editor
Dick Allen, 2010 Contest Judge

CITYLIT
PRESS

Baltimore, Maryland

Library of Congress Control Number: 2011937187

ISBN 978-1-936328-06-2

CityLit Project is a 501(c)(3) Nonprofit Organization
Federal Tax ID Number: 20-0639118

Printed in the United States of America
First Edition

Book Design: Gregg Wilhelm
Book Design Assistance: Jennifer Moss
Cover Photograph: Nicol Sager

CITYLIT
PRESS

c/o CityLit Project
120 S. Curley Street
Baltimore, MD 21224
410.274.5691
www.CityLitProject.org
info@citylitproject.org

Nurturing the culture of literature.

Bits of Sparkling Glass

The term "tour de force" may well occur to you as you read the poems in *Famous*. It did to me. Poem after poem took me in a surprising new direction. I even found myself checking dictionary definitions of "tour de force." Here, I'll paraphrase some: *a brilliant or masterful feat, a notable achievement, a feat of skill, an adroit feat, a feat requiring exceptional strength or virtuosity; something which may have been intentionally undertaken for its difficulty.*

I want to make it clear that I'm using "tour de force" not in its sometimes pejorative sense of being synonymous with a stunt or trick. No, I'm writing of how these poems by Bruce Sager are crafted in order to reward us with new senses of perspective—as only exceptional poetry can do.

In "What I Kept," for instance, Sager takes us through stages of life from grade school to old age. It's masterful, and here's just one of its stanzas:

> I kept the change but lost the dollars, kept a plant
> > until I killed it,
> I kept a woman and then another, I kept a secret
> for almost an hour, I kept in line, I kept good time,
> I kept the rhythm but lost the line, the music was lost
> in the sweep of the hours, the music was lost
> in the Sabbath burning, and still I kept what I kept,
> I kept the Sabbath when I was a child and
> my thoughts were the thoughts of a child

It's not only what's being felt and imaged that's so moving, but the use of rhyme, repetition, and the sure turning from iambs to anapests, the modulations, as the account of a life is distilled onto two pages.

Such feats occur again and again in *Famous*, almost every poem not leaning on others, but strong enough to stand on its own—something not at all that usual in a time of "themed" poetry collections. One example is "The Groundhog," a poem completely different from Richard Eberhart's famous poem with the same title. In Sager's poem, we meet a groundhog exterminator:

> His name was Lester Hackler
> and he wore a three-day growth
> and his words were plain as stubble.

Hackler is successful in killing the groundhog simply, effectively. When the poem ends, he holds up a groundhog corpse very different from Eberhart's transcendent being ("And bones bleaching in the sunlight / Beautiful as architecture"), and hugely more real.

We hear another speaker in "Hitler's Analyst." And in "Jackboot," the poem's narrator goes on a tear associating the word *jackboot* with thing after thing, while "the dryer is clunking with one wet sneaker, / the washer is going, the phone won't stop." And "the parallels / of this world run down the serried stones / of paradise."

Then there's the lovely "A Young Man's Ballad" which fittingly has a young man ask, as do so many, when he shall reach his full potential:

> Perhaps, then, I shall flower at fifty,
> To make my true love proud of me?
>> Nay, lad, time will line thy face,
> And when it does, why, so will she.

Unexpectedly, I found myself accepting the archaic use of "lad" and "flower" and "Nay" and "thy" and was delighted. What audacity to write an old-fashioned poem like this, with old-fashioned language, and *make it work*!

Still elsewhere in these poems, there is even more delight, coupled with that odd way of comparing things peculiar, I sometimes think, only to poets: "for as many hours / as there are doughnuts in a doughnut shop," or "When the electricity came back on" after an outage, "faces fell and our hearts lay / like toads upon the road," or (this is a most quotable poet),

>> Emma is scribbling
> like a crab in a sand pit, and I notice that
> somewhere along the way I seem to have
> fallen in love with the sound of my voice.

and there's "X Marks the Spot" ("How we abuse this little letter") and "Kafka pays a visit," among other romps and acute observations.

Self-conscious, knowledgeable, confident, wacky, exuberant.... Thankfully and fittingly, the poet's bravado is tempered by a winning ability not to take oneself too seriously, as someone with Sager's skills easily could do. This self-deprecation—so useful in the tall-tale teller, the flaunter—is accomplished by irony and exaggeration ("I am myself a cruise / without a name, a blue-grilled bruiser") and even mockery of pretension, as in "The Greatest Poem Ever Written":

> Like a stand-up comic, it has its little jokes.

Finally, well, here's the title of a short poem in which a poet and a fellow drinker are talking: "So what do you do? he asked." And here's part of the answer to the question posed by the poem's title:

> For love, I said, I write poems.
> For love, he said, I shoot birds.
>
> I get up early, I said, for love.
> I get up early, he said, for love.

Love constantly drives these poems. "I love especially the placidity / of the ocean floor," Sager tells us, imagining "Driving Underwater," and parallel lines are "so much in love with The Law / that they slide along like blades in snow," and only with great love of poetry would one create an Abecedarian (if you don't know what one is, look inside), as Sager does in these pages. It is love that creates "The radiance of simple things," Sager's small penultimate poem that praises "the true saying / of what one means."

Such praising is what *Famous* also does, poems sparkling over and over again, "in the flesh," in this most impressive collection.

Dick Allen
Poet Laureate
State of Connecticut

Famous

Famous

Here is the little guy
standing at the top of a dune
so that if you look up at him
all you see is a cut-out against the sky
and all the blue of his eyes
lost in the curtains of that sky.

Here is the band of his swimsuit
grinding against his waist,
here a wet red belt of planets
girdling his middle.

Here is his bucket.
Here are sand crabs scratching.
Here is the thin half-moon
of the handle, the metal settled
into the creases where his palm
flowers into his fingers joyfully,
artfully, mathematically,

flexibly, dependably,
and here is joy, for here
is the little guy standing atop
the light dune of memory
looking down at the woman
rejoicing in the sight of him
now, no longer alarmed
but yet repining, the woman
who has just made his name
bong like a bell through the dunes.

Making film noir

We argue which of us is to sit smoking
over the loud and useless typewriter
knocking back glass after glass
of scotch and which of us

is to go into the street at midday
searching for the undiscovered blonde
who will steal for us like a ghost
through the elegance of midnight.

Driving Underwater

Though you must sacrifice the wind in your hair,
it's really kind of fun, this sort of driving,
once you get the hang of staying in your lane
without the guidance of road stripes
or the familiar coddle of the shoulder.

I love especially the placidity
of the ocean floor,
the red of the urchin
checking the foot's swift descent,

the yellow of the sea fan giving you pause,
the green of the wagging grasses,
their commodious welcome.

Let me tell you, this is a place
where it's okay if you forget your sunglasses,
because sunlight never presents
that much of a problem.

And say what you will about
not being able to roll down the windows,
at least you may tick guano
off your long list of worries.

Is there any downside? you ask.

Of course. Of course.
I would at all times keep an eye out
for those fearsome figures of authority
patrolling the next crevasse.

Surely you know the ones I mean:
the ones who conceal themselves
behind the convenient reef, the ones
whose whole job in the world
seems nothing more, some days,
than giving chase to pull you over
for a salty, sharp-toothed chat.

So keep a low profile. Don't startle
if you happen suddenly upon one or two
sleek silhouettes sheltering in the coral,
and bear in mind that often
they prowl in pairs, submerged
in deep conversation
for as many hours
as there are doughnuts in a doughnut shop.

Since it's hard to get up a head of steam
against the resistance of so much water,
you'll have all the time you need
to enjoy the ribbons of flora and fauna
whose sole industry appears to reside
in the creation of fantastical displays right,
left, above and (occasionally) below you.

And if you should happen to bump into
another driver, rest easy: at a hefty 2 m.p.h.,
neither of you is about to create much paperwork
for the insurance people.

As to the question of deep water driving . . .

well, catching the current behind a speeding whale
can be exhilarating, I'll be the first to admit it.
And it's easy on the tank, especially
in a venue where the next filling station
is more a prayer than a promise.

But I must caution you about the risky practice
of actually driving *between* two whales.

And I am not speaking of those dappled
twelve foot orca with which even
the most modest of dolphinaria
seem to be stocked these days.

I am talking about the great
behemoths of myth and literature, the bible
black leviathan whose single painful thrash
in the lithograph of an old book
can be seen to capsize
two or three longboats' worth of men
a thousand miles from home.

I am talking about
the great cresting of the waters
the eyes and hair of Jonah
and the bounteous belly of the beast.

Thamnophis sirtalis

You could call it that.

Or recovered from the startle
of a silver river
running by your ankle,
the shirred skin,
you could come down
from your high horse
and call it a garter snake.

Some of us, though, must take the oar
of reason in one hand and the oar
of allocution in the other
to pull hard against
the risen waves of fear.

It is these who will name
names and create
a descending order,
classification
serving as poultice,
a slowing of the pulse:
Animalia, Chordata, Reptilia,
Squamata, Serpentes,
on and on drones Linnaeus

as you imagine your own descent
into the silver waters of a river
opening in the unmown grasses
of this life, your own
back yard, the great chaos,
the great calm.

When the electricity
went out

How romantic, we thought, as the numbers
on the clock faded into the night table
and were gone.

The blades of the fan slowed and slowed
and then there was nothing moving,
nothing to tell time by

except whatever might be splashing
inside us, native, ecstatic, like children
caught at midnight dipping in a lake.

When the electricity
came back on

How prosaic, we thought, as the numbers
on the clock blinked from its face
like an ad for Genesis.

The blades of the fan revved and revved
until all the room was moving,
nothing but time going by

and papers lifting, dust, feathers, our
faces fell and our hearts lay
like toads upon the road.

There are sixty words
for *fish*,
fifty-five
for *frozen*,
but *fax, syndrome* and
return on investment
are nowhere
to be found.

Mardloralik
sleeps with
two wives.

Sarápoq
glitters
with moisture.

Pátagtorpoq
beats its wings
together.

There are *magic*,
frostbite,
boring a hole.

The words for
food and *work*
make echoes.

In a land that lies
between hard covers,
snow, sky and torrent
issue in stasis, rivers freeze
in the act of surge

and the bodies of fish
belie cool fire
in the bellies of men
who have stood
the deep cold
to catch them.

Abecedarian Concerns

i.   a – b – a – b – c – d – c – d
I'll come right at you through your open eyes.
The more you read the less you'll understand.
Good luck in rousing justice where it lies.
Bend closer. See my cursive? It's just grand.
The pages *burn*, you say? I'll bet they do . . . .
My fictions? Just like life. Both full of crap.
Come spend an hour with the Dancing Jew.
If you want something easy, take a nap.

ii.   d – d – a – a – b – b – c – c
My fictions? Just like life. Both full of crap.
If you want something easy, take a nap.
Good luck in rousing justice where it lies.
I'll come right at you through your open eyes.
Bend closer. See my cursive? It's just grand.
The more you read the less you'll understand.
Come spend an hour with the Dancing Jew.
The pages *burn*, you say? I'll bet they do . . . .

iii.   b – d – d – b – c – a – a – c
Bend closer. See my cursive? It's just grand.
If you want something easy, take a nap.
My fictions? Just like life. Both full of crap.
The more you read the less you'll understand.
The pages *burn*, you say? I'll bet they do . . . .
Good luck in rousing justice where it lies.
I'll come right at you through your open eyes.
Come spend an hour with the Dancing Jew.

iv.　d – d – c – c
Eyes crap,
grand nap.
Understand, Jew,
lies do . . . .

Jackboot

We're talking. It's a comfy domestic scene,
or should be. But our dogs are making us
crazy over the neighbor's riding mower,
the dryer is clunking with one wet sneaker,
the washer is going, the phone won't stop.
*Jack*boot, you say? Now *that's* a strange word
for a twelve-year-old. Just what are they
teaching in history class these days?

My daughter smiles at my Sunday sprawl
and opens her notebook on the floor.
Her quill is poised like a dart. Jackboot.
She requires a definition. She needs it now.
I can see she wants me to pour out my heart
while she scribbles like a monitor needle.
And jackboot should be easy, something
I read up on somewhere not so long ago,
but somehow, it's crazy, I can't quite
remember: I'm thinking Nazis maybe.

Well, I say out loud, I believe the jackboot
to be a figure of speech, unless it happens
to be an *actual* jackboot . . . and yes, good
question, this shows you're thinking, it *could*
mean both at the same time. And why not?
Why not go strutting in jackboots while
barking your orders and acting the bully?
Though that would be quite beyond the pale,
and honey, I've been there, I *know* the pale –
a fence that the English set up for the Irish,

a boundary of stakes and posts they created
to mark off order from chaos. Nothing
you'd want your boot to venture beyond
whether jack, black or snickety-snack . . .

. . . but I can see that this venturing is a little
beyond her pale even as the jackboot is a
little beyond mine, yet why should that stop
so learned a disquisition? – so I move on
to answer a follow-up question, explaining
that I can't exactly at this moment say with
any real precision *precisely* what a figure
of speech is, not any more than she might
say what a jackboot is, but that's okay,
we could look it up if I were not lying here
so heavy in the weight of all my seasons,

and I say this smiling up at her and she is
writing it all down, she is scribbling like
a frog on a pond as I nod yes, there are
surely occasions that call for jackboots,
that you might find yourself, for instance,
slipping into a very good pair – heels still
muddied from a recent duel – while dressing
for the governor's ball, but then again
the term could be a mere instruction,
a suggestion, as in what to wear when
you bury a beanstalk, jackboot, jackboot,
frankly, sweetie, I'm a little fuzzy on this,
but in no way should it be confused with
standard footwear, so forget the clodhopper
and the cleat, forget the sneak, and besides,
I would prefer to spend our time together

chatting about filial duty, not jackboots,
and Emma appears to be on the same page –
she's stolidly taking dictation, I see, and
I think of a leaf scribbling on a sidewalk.

The best figure for fealty and obduracy
remains the law of numbers, I say blindly,
sensing my words pouring out of her fingers,
for parallel lines must run forever abreast
    (and isn't that a splendid image? –
    right out of Euclid, as I recall),
right past the roof and the telephone lines
that rule the skies like notebook paper,
two lines so much in love with The Law
that they slide along like blades in snow,
gulag to galaxy, two huskies in harness,
geometry's compass, and if that's not love,
I ask you, what is? Emma is scribbling
like a crab in a sand pit, and I notice that
somewhere along the way I seem to have
fallen in love with the sound of my voice.

Somewhere in the back alley of history,
meanwhile, a man in jackboots mugs a man
with a walking stick, and the parallels
of this world run down the serried stones
of paradise. They enrich its plentiful puddles
with such a touching devotion that even
Milton's daughters look up from their labors
a moment – near nameless and thankless
they are, wringing their hands with fatigue
and cracking their knuckles, fed up, lost
and bored, and thinking heaven knows
what, but surely not father knows best.

X Marks the Spot

How we abuse this little letter.

Like a pick-up in an unlit room,
made to mean
whatever we need it to mean
at any given moment –
a target, for example.

Or the unrecognized term in an equation,
the nameless hero who never gets
to meet the King of Sweden;
the rejection of an idea
in a draft, on a list; or punched over
a circle to mean *not*; finagled
to depict, above the eyes, a knock-out
in the comics; but also the promise
of treasure squirreled just so many paces
from the Grandpappy Oak,
entombed on a tiny island.

X permits the unlettered to tell us
who they were, or are, to sign
their lives away, to convey what they have
of the riches of this world; yet
will alternate with *O* in tendering
affection epistolary, e- or snail.

Always we put whatever face
the moment calls for
upon this cross little letter
whose story might have been
about Xanadu (but Coleridge had
done it already) or Xavier Cugat
or good King Xerxes, even the
brilliant craftsman X. J. Kennedy –
the list echoes with etceteras –

but better to make it a celebration
of the unknown, the lusted-after,
the factor that keeps us rolling
against the night.

The Three Wishes

A small string band,
the civility of crystal.

I approached her
from behind. She felt
my fingers upon her waist.

Always there is the one
who makes the request,
and always the one
who must reply, whatever
the question: the echo.

I wanted to force her
to reveal herself, to
answer, to grant, to say
yes, something has rubbed me
the right way, and here I am
now, just for you,
shiny as a silver dollar.

Are you the First Wish? I asked.

She turned then, darkening.

You've mistaken me for my sister.
We're really nothing alike.
She's the one holding court
on the couch, surrounded
by all those tuxedos.

My other sister?
Back there, leaning on the piano.
The looker in the push-up bra
giggling at everything, suffering
every fool with
a touch of gladness
and drinking
a little more gin
than she can handle.

I smiled at her.

Then you must be
the Third Wish.
The coup de grâce.

She looked like a butterfly
pinned to a page.

I am nothing, you must waste me,
she said. *I am the one*
you must throw
upon the water.

The Groundhog

We paid one hundred fifty dollars
for the man to come
to trap the groundhog.

The man was simple as his math.
Simple, meaning plain. Clear.
What you see is what you get.

His name was Lester Hackler
and he wore a three-day growth
and his words were plain as stubble.

Them sumbitches get under your porch
and dig away half the foundation
and then whaddaya got?

A hole under the porch.
Eleven days later he came by
and held up the jaws of death

looking like the jaws of a shark
and the freshly dead groundhog
dangled against a backdrop

of brick and oak. That was it.
There was very little geometry to it.
What you see is what you get.

Morphemes

The endless pairing of appositives
becomes oppressive, duty pulls
like a lexicon. The sorting wants some
shake, some shimmer, a little jazz,
the brainless flutter and flash
of a school of fish, rudderless.

All aging is a sort of training, a trial
of square pegs upon the Roman track
of valor, of fits that startle and stop,
of serendipity itself, as *Homo sapiens
sapiens* tastes *neanderthalensis* just under
his frontal lobes. Here the place where

musing & music & lingo collide, give up
the ghost, surrender the Me – just fish
in a school of fish. I am myself a cruise
without a name, a blue-gilled bruiser
bezeled and jeweled beneath the break
of the sacred waters, a holy gill

composing some molecules with care
within my makeup mirror. My scales
make color, my color music, a raw
mascara remarks a steady sun. Yet
the sun is nothing without its threat
of ice, the pulsing scales wink out

like albinos scotching their hides
on a beach. So much the better. So
much for whimsy's dictates. I long
for the abc of the school yard, queuing
by choice, at times by chance, long
blueprints gone in the daylong tides.

Recital

You are the dew on the morning grass
and the burning wheel of the sun.
                    BILLY COLLINS

You are the dew on the morning grass
and the burning wheel of the sun.
You are the a-ok and the thumbs up,
the pilot smiling broadly from his cockpit,
the movie star flashing her white teeth
while the photographers roil with excitement,
the robin sitting on her eggs
and the cardinal leading a choir boy
into the cool elegance of his chambers.

I am the choir boy dragging into the chambers
as well as a little wart on the side of Eichmann's nose,
a warm glass of Coke, last year's cell phone model.

You might also find it instructive to learn
that I am a cell phone from the year before that,
and so on, going all the way back to a time
when portable communication was as large
as the image of the megaphone moving over the sea
that you stole from Ferlinghetti. Ferlinghetti,
I might point out in passing, is also a wart
on the side of a nose, but not the sort of nose
you find on just any face, I mean a nose
that can sniff out the trouble with poetry
and snort out a litany of prescriptive relief.

Meanwhile, I remain neither the moon in the trees
motionless in time, releasing twig by twig
the night-entangled branches, nor the trees themselves
coddling the robin gently tending her eggs.
No way I tend eggs gently. I may, however,
be the stone in an aging troubadour's throat
or a field of cornflower pollen commanding a sneeze.

But don't worry, I'm not the burning wheel of the sun.
You are still the burning wheel of the sun.
You will always be the burning wheel of the sun,
not to mention the stage lights and – somehow –
    the stage.

Hitler's Analyst

There are so many ways
we could go from here.

We could dissemble. We could invent. We could write,
which is, of course, to lie.

We could avoid the topic entirely,
a tribute to Frank O'Hara, a paean to misdirection.

We could blather about schnitzel and beer
while the cattle rumble past in the background;
or, in a few lines, ape disingenuous Wilbur –
we could focus on the innocuous, a merchant's household
in Graz, plain as paste – anything but the torturous belt
of Alois, from whose direct line, from whose leather
we might trace the wobbling borders of Europe.

Does this stand so much as a chance
of being about Hitler's analyst?

With guards at the doors, with sirens on the roof,
with overstuffed generals outflanking each other
in the anterooms, the inner sanctum will brim
with courtesies of the teacup; two steps
and we're in the Old World again, outside a square
in Siena, or hanging grotesque from a balcony;
the mind, it trips where flesh is shy to wander.

So here we sit, Herr Hitler yakking away
about the Academy, the wonders of watercolor.

What fine cloth
his clothing is made of.

What if you had been a better painter? asks a fool
and the guards come stiffly to attention,
the admirable butch of the rifle, but the little general
lets it slide, he smiles, and now we are on to chopping
wood in the autumn, and Vermeer, the softness
of his line, the difficult nurture of show dogs,
fashions in the Prussian mustache. Anything, really.

Someone is taking notes. *How does that
make you feel?* he inquires, and then begins
a furious scribble. And who's to say
what the old fiend would answer
if we let him. But of course
we'd let him.

Memory's a stream always running towards a mouth.

Somewhere from the north comes a little rain
and a few springs rise into the first notes of a symphony
that will in due course thunder upon the Rhine.

The devil, meanwhile, takes Aunt Johanna
against the fine latticework in the back garden
of a splendid summer home deep in the Austrian green.
He works her like a porn star, her skirts are tossed
like a small province overrun by panzer.

In poetry the sun is always shining
unless it's raining. The possibilities are endless.

And like all talk, like tanks, in fact, track always
towards this unreachable border.

Kafka pays a visit

He has wonderful manners. Whenever he drops in
he makes sure to locate whatever looks to be the freshest
pile of papers on my desk, and then, with a quizzical
expression, asks if he might read over whatever it is
that I have been filling them with. Oh please, Franz,
why in the world would you want to do that? This is
nothing but week-old baloney to you . . . I only wish
I could offer a little filet. Some tea would be nice, he says,
deftly abandoning the world of metaphor for the world
of thirst. I call upstairs. Honey, I say, Franz is here, and
could we trouble you for a little tea? Kafka busies himself
in the meantime puttering with my pages, and every so
often he hums or coughs a little and then realizes that his
hum or cough is making me anxious, so he follows up
with "This is very good, this part" or "I especially like
what you've done right here," but it's all a little game,
I know that as his eyes are wandering over the papers
his ears are attuned to the steps, and sure enough, a couple
of minutes later there is a creak on the stairs and my wife
appears, first the strong calves, then the thighs, the waist,
the animal breasts, and I see it just the way Franz sees it.
He always has a few nice words for her. She always blushes.
It's no secret among us, the reason for these visits.

A Young Man's Ballad

Perhaps, then, I shall flower at twenty,
To make my elders proud of me?
      Nay, lad, twenty's young for that,
A world of time the world to see.

Perhaps, then, I shall flower at thirty,
To make my comrades proud of me?
      Nay, lad, the rich will have none of it
And the poor ones beg the heart from thee.

Perhaps, then, I shall flower at forty,
To make my tutors proud of me?
      Nay, lad, there they'll lie a'sleeping,
Even as Christ at thirty-three.

Perhaps, then, I shall flower at fifty,
To make my true love proud of me?
      Nay, lad, time will line thy face,
And when it does, why, so will she.

Perhaps, then, I shall flower at sixty,
To make my townsmen proud of me?
      Nay, lad, there's a wall between;
They'll only see what they will see.

Perhaps, then, I shall flower at seventy,
To make my children proud of me?
      Nay, lad, a father's deeds are fond –
They'll long to be rid of thee.

Perhaps, then, I shall flower at eighty,
To make the wide world proud of me?
        Yea, lad, ye shall flower at eighty,
And gladden the grass and the tumbling bee.

You could not be more beautiful

When you wear your hair like that
(you hear me think)
you are so beautiful
you remind me of Cleopatra

If you had hair
(I hear you think)
you would be a little more beautiful
than you are now

If you were more beautiful
(we hear each other think)
than you are now,
ach, the grief it would cause

As Antony gave away Cyprus
and Crete and old Cyrene,
gave in to the fingers of love,
what we would give away –

our persons in all their parts

our persons in all their parts
like clouds in a smoky bar
along a Nile of beer
and under the boozy stars

a jukebox of earthly delights
for I have been crisp as a shirtsleeve
you have been soft as a thong
and the night has been gentle

and we have been gentle
so gentle with each other
but where is the proof of beauty
if not in a country song

The light struck the dying pharaoh
in such a way, just so
You could not be more beautiful
(we each think to ourselves)

(we each think to ourselves)

What I kept

I left grade school and I kept a picture of the Miss America man
      Bert Parks squatting next to me in the school yard,
      he was wearing the mask of minor celebrity, I was
      wearing rabbit ears and a dab of paint on the tip of
      my nose, I kept a notion of the absurd and a vague
      recollection of the weather the day absurdity came
I left high school and I kept a packet of Algebra tests that all say
      "100" across the top, I kept the nausea of existential decay
      and a library copy of Roget, I kept a yearbook with a roadmap
      to my failures, their long Sixties hair and their brilliant eyes
I left Johns Hopkins early and I kept my tail between my legs, I left
      over objections and the Dean of Students asked me why
      and I kept my mouth shut, and as for the real reasons I left,
      they kept to the shadows the trees made on the Quad
Father died and I kept the Zeiss binoculars and his colored ribbons
      from the war, I kept his undersized golf jacket that would
      fit if only I lost a little weight, I kept the scar on my
      fourth finger from my experiment with his band saw
Mother died and I kept the two spooky porcelain miniatures
      she played with back in the Twenties when she was a girl,
      the world was roaring and she was playing with dolls
      and when people ask me why I have dolls in my office
      sometimes I walk to the shelves and hand them over
      with caution, warning about the fragility of their limbs
The basement flooded and I kept the mildew in the corners
      and the damp stains running around the walls, I kept
      a box of poems that were no good and now stick
      together like men smoking outside an employment office,

I kept all of the ideas I could scrape from the boxes
and I kept some scraps of paper from the repairs, here,
I said to my wife, these are receipts, keep 'em, I kept
all of nature's wet palette when it marches on a home
I kept the hole in my insides where my gall bladder once squeezed
out its awful juices, I kept the acid brush of time and
painted my face year in, year out, I kept out of the way
of trouble and so I made it to my sixth decade, I kept
quiet, I kept up, step, watch, bad company, house
I kept at it and at it, I kept going, I kept off the grass unless
no one was looking, and I kept my temper and, at times,
the peace, but the peace can be hard to keep, I kept
the end in sight, the end always keeps, I kept a diary
but one day it was full and I didn't buy another,
I kept my seat unless an old person was standing,
and most times I kept my job, but not always
I kept the change but lost the dollars, kept a plant until I killed it,
I kept a woman and then another, I kept a secret
for almost an hour, I kept in line, I kept good time,
I kept the rhythm but lost the line, the music was lost
in the sweep of the hours, the music was lost
in the Sabbath burning, and still I kept what I kept,
I kept the Sabbath when I was a child and
my thoughts were the thoughts of a child
I kept a light on until it flamed, I kept up on the notion of light,
I kept my word when I learned to keep it, I kept
a list of how many times I'd broken something
and how many times I'd had something broken,
but it's not really a good list to keep, one day
I lost it and after that I kept the tally to myself.

Footnote

Well, you know that writers lie.
Some is true history, some gray,
some is made up from whole cloth
for the sake of the narrative.

There was no flood in the cellar.
And I never kept the Sabbath.
But the part about Bert Parks
is entirely true. (The paint was
tough to remove. Mom had to
scrub and scrub.) As for dad,
the man would not have known
a band saw from a band stand,
the chance of his owning one
would have been the same as
a comet hitting the west wing
of the White House at exactly
ten after two this afternoon.

And killing Millard Fillmore.

Perhaps more slender still.

The Greatest Poem Ever Written

No bells, confetti, archangels joyed its arrival.
The stars were normal that day. Traffic ran fine.
Nobody stood in a manger. Nobody stood in a line.

Couplet, quatrain, sestina, sequence . . .
people have puzzled for eons over its form.
Whenever a scholar waves flags of triumph
hogs run wild from its ruined gardens.
It suffers no rhymes, except by fluke;
but one afternoon when the hogs got loose
a child discovered that each word rhymes.
Like a stand-up comic, it has its little jokes.
Alliteration, metonymy, elision have crept
between its lines like summer weeds.
And simile it's gobbled like a fruit.

Dictated by an after-dinner drunk, its shire of birth
is unremembered. A secretary took down every note
but the words came fast. In spots she used her own.
It plays like a radio or a lute, fast, loose, some say
its punctuation echoes the crack of a bone.

Today we track it like a satellite.
People make careers of it.
We know it's real as a cave in Zion.
We know it's real as a marriage vow.
We know it wakes to a different mouth each morning.
We know it works in the dawn, it works in the dark.

It works for a marriage, a tribe, a nation. We know
it means the same thing in Cyrillic, Chinese, Greek.
But like the moon, or vulgar gestures, its meanings shift
from place to place. It doesn't dress up or take on airs.
It doesn't paint its face. It isn't much of a celebration.
At times it seems like nothing, an offhand remark.

So what do you do? he asked

For money or love? I replied.
He surprised me: For love.
For love, I said, I write poems.
For love, he said, I shoot birds.

I get up early, I said, for love.
I get up early, he said, for love.
I sit for hours and nothing happens
we each said at the same time.

He looked down into his drink.
I'm sick of shooting birds, he said.
I looked down into my drink.
I hear that, friend, I answered.

The radiance of simple things

How oxygen will
occasionally flush
the sedentary lung,
full of its yellow portents,

and morning flash
over an eastern hill
with no other meaning
tucked in its pants
than its own
simple self.

What a gift, the true saying
of what one means,
in the flesh.

Walking with my heart

I put my arm around him.
Old chum, I say,
it's been years since I've seen you
on my sleeve. Is anything
the matter?

My heart looks at me with eyes
weightless as the Buddha's.
He gestures towards the sea,
the dead things
within it.

Because he has no tongue
he cannot speak.
And after all these years
I know better than
to interpret.

I cannot guess what you mean,
I say, as we turn back,
as we turn to face
where we've come from,
our footprints dusty on the esplanade.

Acknowledgments

The Who's: Clarinda Harriss is a luminous presence on the country's literary scene. This series of publications is named in her honor, sponsored and published by CityLit Press. Thanks go to Gregg A. Wilhelm, Executive Director of the CityLit Project in residence at the University of Baltimore, to Dr. Michael Salcman, series editor of the annual Clarinda Harriss Poetry Prize, and to the distinguished and much decorated poet, editor and professor who served as final judge for the 2010 contest, Dick Allen, currently Poet Laureate of the state of Connecticut.

Recognition and Disclosure: Nary a one of these poems has had much of a social life; they all debut here and now. "Making Film Noir" and "Footnote" and "You could not be more beautiful" and "Walking with my heart" have been added to the original (judged) manuscript; the author stands solely responsible for their inclusion.

A Model T: There was some trifling debate – more a cordial discussion than an uncivil controversy – about what to name this little collection. The central image of the poem "Famous" seemed happily, even mysteriously, harmonious with the photo on the front cover, and so gave us our title. But another intriguing choice which could easily be coupled with that image (created, incidentally, by the poet's wife, and capturing their young son on the shores of Lahaina) is the poem "Driving Underwater," also appearing in these pages. So, before it slips away beneath the waves of a comfy obscurity, if you wish to very quietly, very privately rename this modest production after rummaging through the drawers of that alternative poem, go right ahead: driving underwater, after all, describes writing poetry to a T.

Bruce Sager lives in Westminster, Maryland, and works as a corporate officer in a systems integration firm. He has been the recipient of Maryland State Arts Council Individual Artist Awards in both fiction (2008) and poetry (2011), a Baltimore City Arts Grant in poetry (1987), and the 1986 Artscape Literary Arts Award in poetry, judged by William Stafford. Prior chapbooks include *Nine Ninety-Five* (1971) and *The Pumping Station* (1986).

CITYLIT
PRESS

CityLit Press's mission is to provide a venue for writers who might otherwise be overlooked by larger publishers due to the literary nature or regional focus of their projects. It is the imprint of nonprofit CityLit Project, founded in Baltimore in 2004.

CityLit nurtures the culture of literature in Baltimore and throughout Maryland by creating enthusiasm for literature, building a community of avid readers and writers, and opening opportunities for young people and diverse audiences to embrace the literary arts.

Thank you to our major supporters: the Maryland State Arts Council, the Baltimore Office of Promotion and The Arts, and the Baltimore Community Foundation. More information and documentation is available at www.guidestar.org.

Additional support is provided by individual contributors. Financial support is vital for sustaining the ongoing work of the organization. Secure, online donations can by made at our web site (click on "Donate").

CityLit is a member of the Greater Baltimore Cultural Alliance, the Maryland Association of Nonprofit Organizations, and the Writers' Conferences and Centers division of the Association of Writers and Writing Programs (AWP).

For submission guidelines, information about CityLit Press's poetry chapbook contests, and all the programs and services offered by CityLit, please visit www.citylitproject.org.

Harriss Poetry Prize

Launched in 2009, the Harriss Poetry Prize is named in honor of Clarinda Harriss, eminent Baltimore poet, publisher, and professor of English at Towson University. Harriss, educated at Johns Hopkins University and Goucher College, is a widely published, award-winning poet and she serves as editor/director of BrickHouse Books, Maryland's oldest literary press.

2010 Judge: Dick Allen
2009 Judge: Michael Salcman

For complete guidelines, please go to www.citylit-project.org and click on "CityLit Press." Send entry fee, manuscript with table of contents, acknowledgments, and two coversheets (one with name, title, mailing address, daytime phone, and email address and one with *title only*) to:

Harriss Poetry Prize
CityLit Press
c/o CityLit Project
120 S. Curley Street
Baltimore, MD 21224

Annual submission deadline is October 1 (postmarked).